CURIOUS FRUITS VEGETABLES

❊

An Aleatoric Abecedary of Floral Fauna

BY JIM COUGHENOUR

Deviled Tongue

SAN FRANCISCO | CALIFORNIA | MMXII

DEVILED TONGUE CHAPBOOK Nº 1

COPYRIGHT © 2012 BY JIM COUGHENOUR

ALL RIGHTS RESERVED.

DESIGN BY NICHOLAS PAVKOVIC

ISBN 978-0-9838757-0-3

Deviled Tongue

SAN FRANCISCO | CALIFORNIA | WWW.DEVILEDTONGUE.COM

L'invitation au dommage

Each character contained herein
Embodies a unique chagrin.
Judge them gently. Are they queerer
Than encounters in your mirror?
Come celebrate the human curse.
Enjoy these escapades in verse.

Aunt Aubergine

—

Aunt Aubergine is sweetly shy,
She'll never look you in the eye;
Yet with a sideways, saw-toothed grin,
Invites you to commit a sin.

—

Blackberry Buck

Blackberry Buck is out of luck.
His inner child has run amuck.
He's seedy, stained and overripe.
Unpicked, Buck is nobody's type.

MEAT = MURDER
I ONLY EAT
HUMAN VEGETABLES

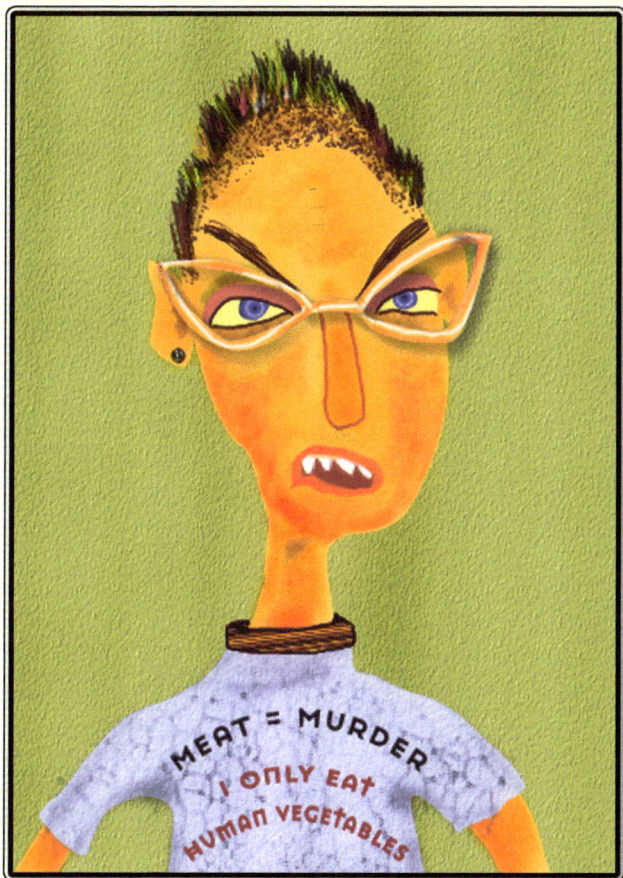

Chad Chicory

Chad Chicory's in ecstasy
Epatering les bourgeoisie
Warm, earnest, unerotic folks
Are shocked by Chad's psychotic jokes.

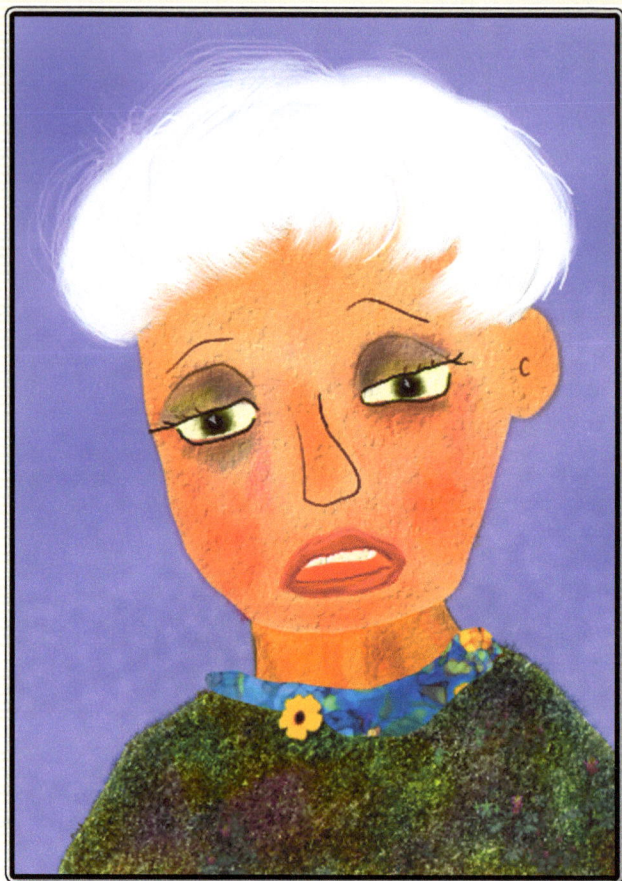

Dot Dandelion

———

Dot Dandelion's dog has passed.
Perhaps she'll try a man at last?
"Too hard to train," Dot shakes her head.
"A man's best trick is playing dead."

———

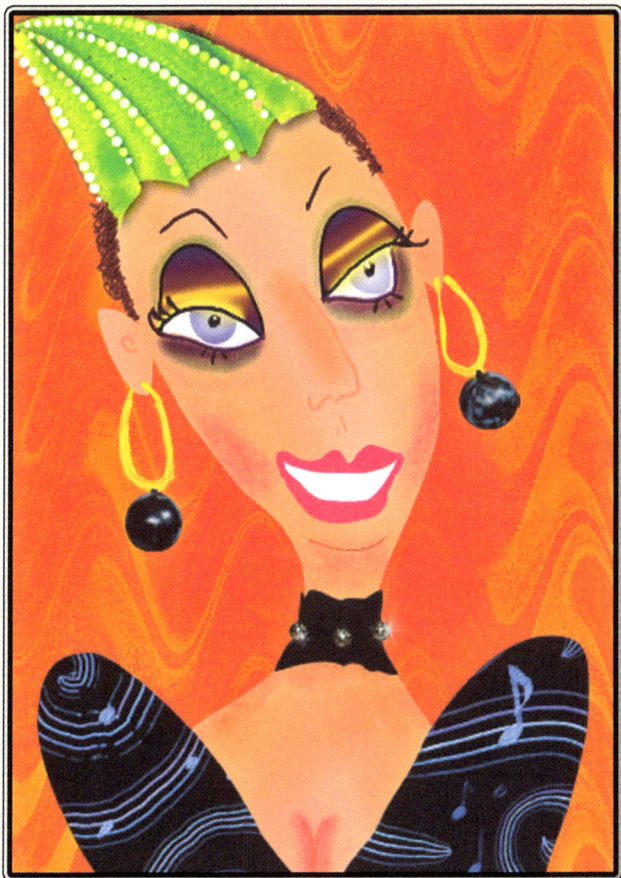

Edina Endive

Edina Endive, ectomorph,
Once entertained a circus dwarf.
She tricked him out like Halloween,
Then, as a treat, turned trampoline.

Fred Fig

Fred Fig prefers the fetid air
Of skater boys in underwear.
His gustatory joy's complete
When nibbling at their fusty feet.

Guava Gwen

—◆—

Guava Gwen, of peppery tongue,
Erupts with umbrage at the young.
Their frolic fills her with chagrin.
Will no one love this grimalkin?

—◆—

Harry Horseradish

———◆———

Harry Horseradish looks so flushed.

What's wrong? I cried.

He said, I'm crushed. Dismayed – reduced – by words obscene:

My sweetheart says I taste hircine.

———◆———

Iceberg Lettice

Iceberg Lettice is so refined
She lives entirely in her mind.
Admirers who get physical
Are chilled by eyes most quizzical.

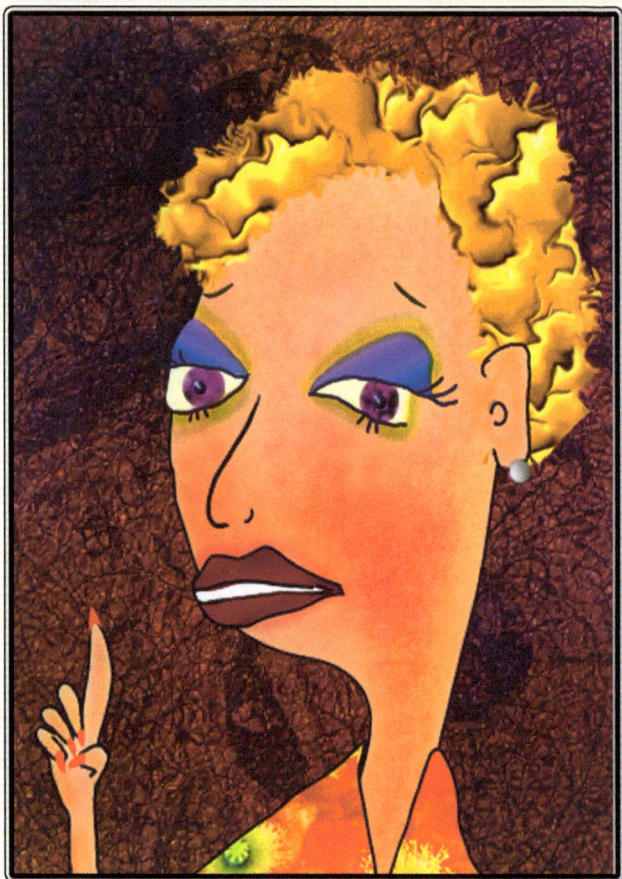

Heidi Jicama

Heidi Jicama has no clue
What draws her to didgeridoo.
It isn't just – she's quick to say –
Its ithyphallic shape per se.

Kumquat Ken

—◆—

Kumquat Ken is in a pickle –
Lust dissolved, libido fickle –
Stunned to find his precious gherkin
Won't be parted from her merkin.

—◆—

The Lemon Lady

The Lemon Lady scares me too.
She stalks the night in shrouds of blue.
When fog untwines her tangled hair,
She stumbles home for solitaire.

Marvin Marrow

Marvin Marrow knows in his bones
He'll never repay all his loans.
Nor will he be forever young...
Bankrupt, washed-up: his life is dung.

Nina Nettle

Nina Nettle's in fine fettle –
Shaved her schnoz and skipped the shtetl,
Went platinum and acted goy,
Then landed her a Jewish boy.

Orlando Okra

*Orlando Okra can't decide
If she's a groom — or he's a bride.
Transgendered love's mixed stratagem
Is M2F or F2M?*

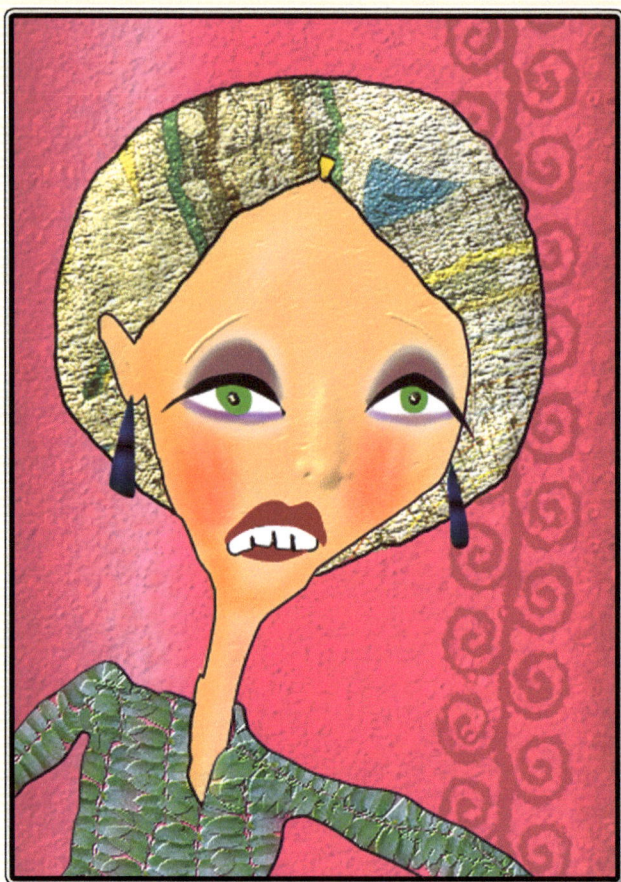

Peggy Parsnip

Peggy Parsnip popped six pink pills:
Three for depression, three for thrills.
Bipolar toward all things she craves –
By night she weeps, by day she raves.

Quentin Quince

—————

Quentin Quince is his own reward;
His amour propre is untoward.
It's true, he is nine-parts pretense,
Yet at his core, he's quite intense.

—————

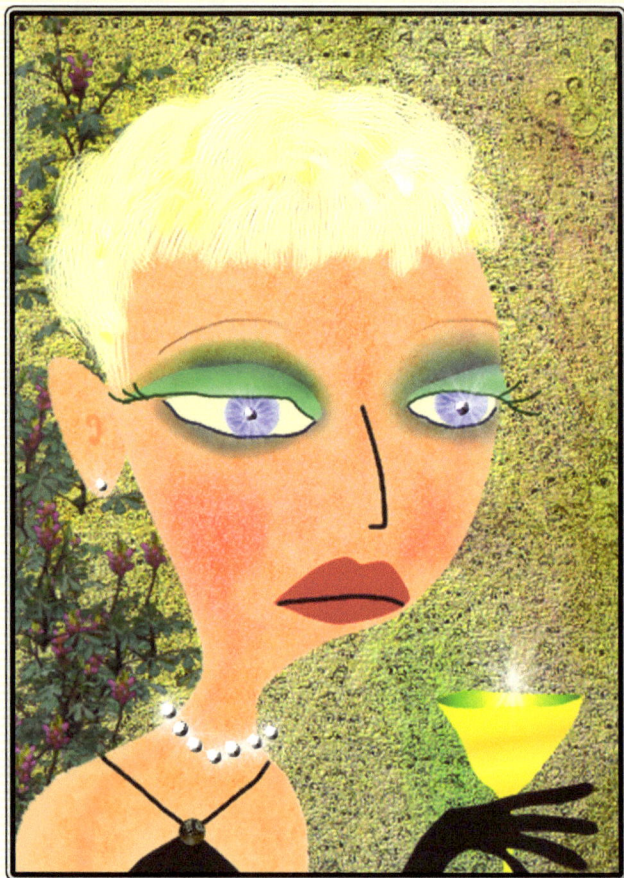

Renata van Radicchio

—◆—

Renata van Radicchio
Will not engage in quid pro quo.
Like some marauding blonde corsair
She leaves her lovers fleeced and bare.

—◆—

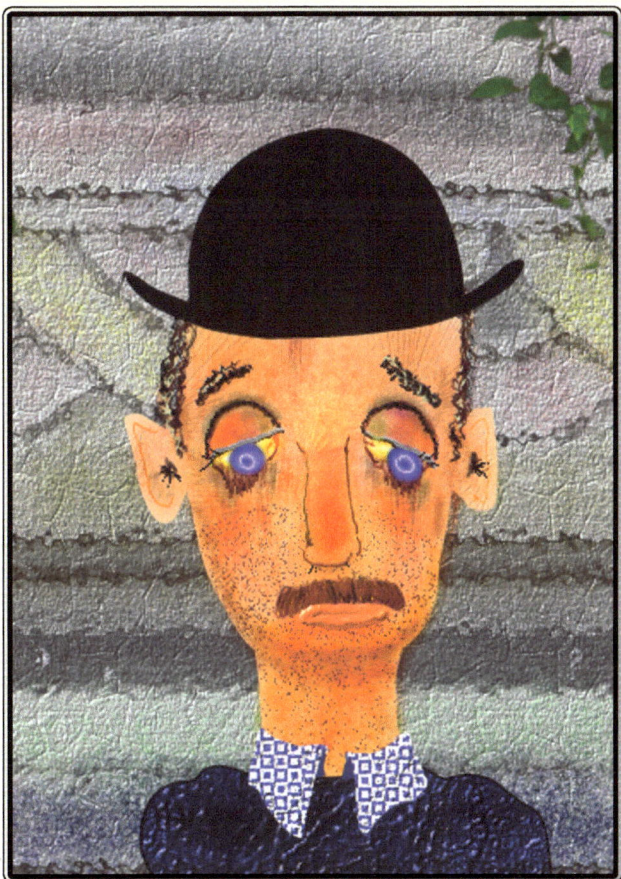

Sidney Shallot

—

Sidney Shallot, worn-out roué,
Will not attend tonight's soiree.
His medication makes him hard
But leaves him feeling rather charred.

Tonya Tamarind

Tonya Tamarind's so authentic
That she's never photogenic.
Embittered, mad, morose, or stewed,
She will inflict her savage mood.

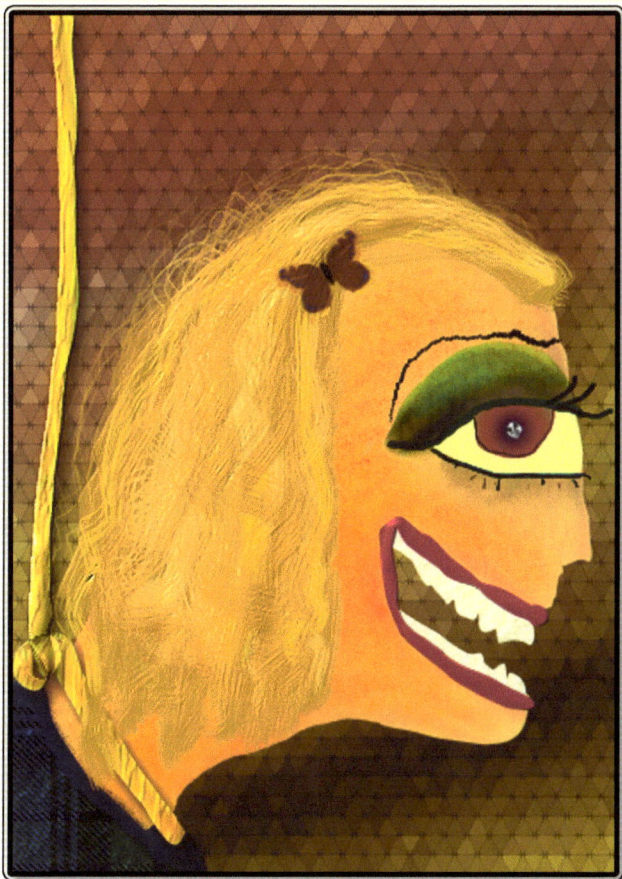

Ursula Ugli

Ursula Ugli takes fierce pride
In fantasies of suicide.
"My chi exults in exercise —
Inventing ultimate goodbyes."

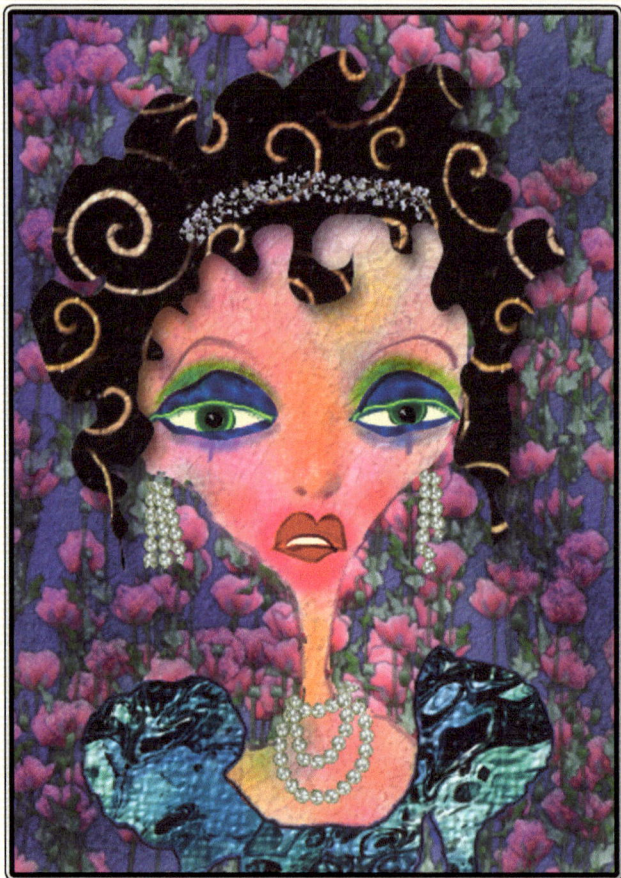

Velvet Apple

—

Velvet Apple adopts the mien
Of flowers fragrant and vespertine.
The face she wears looks best at night.
(It takes eight hours to get it right.)

—

Walt Watercress

—

Walt Watercress, that noble mess,
Unwisely opted to confess.
Sometimes the truth should not be shared;
What Walt undid can't be repaired.

—

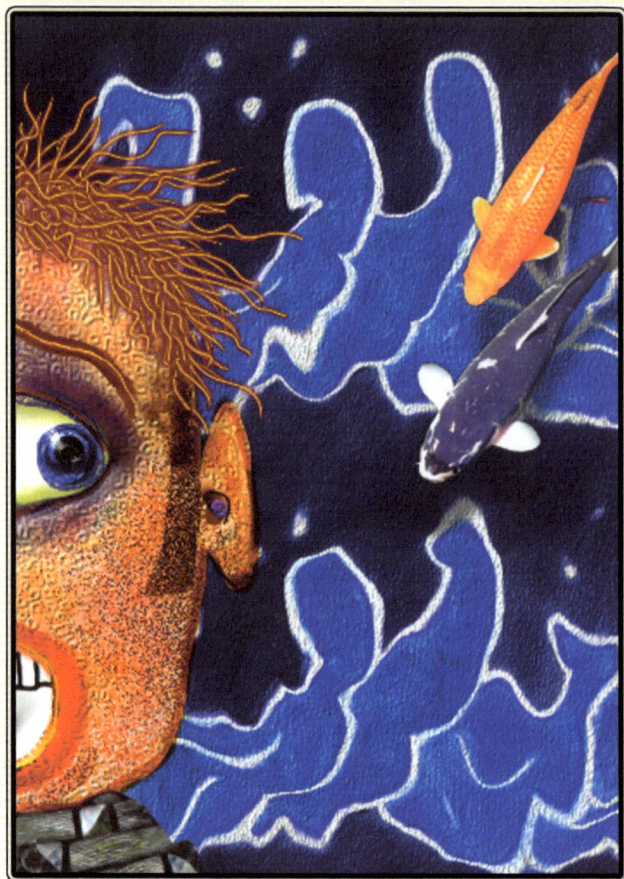

Xerxes Xylocarp

Xerxes Xylocarp screams at fish.
His face evokes a petri dish.
To him the world's a cruel façade
That can't disguise the sport of God.

Yolanda Yam

Yolanda Yam can't understand
Why things have not turned out as planned.
She'd meant to be chic, svelte and wise,
Not drunk at home with thunder thighs.

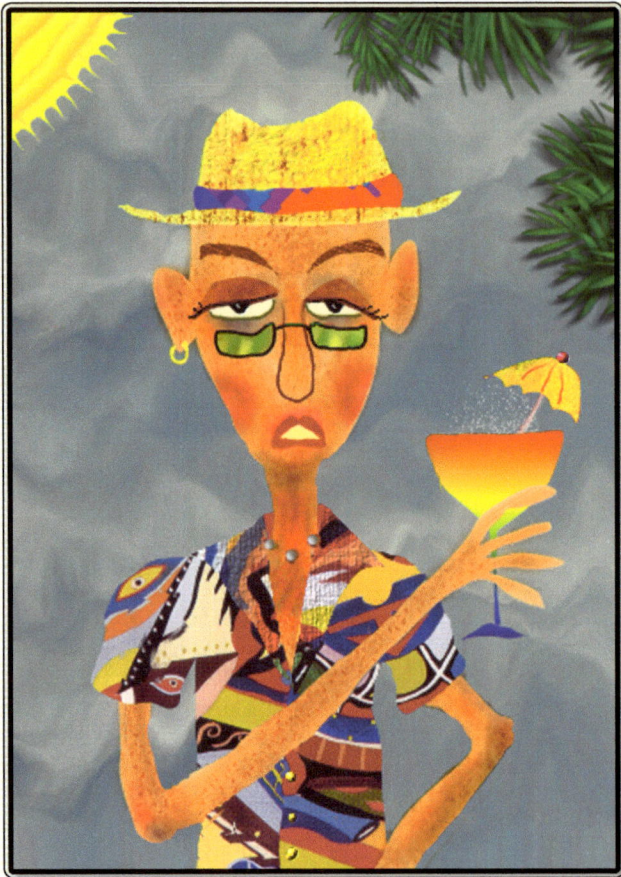

Zack Zapote

Zack Zapote is not gay.
He's "civilized," he claims, not fey.
Thus his taste for lads plebeian
Merely proves he's "European."

www.ingramcontent.com/pod-product-compliance
Lightning Source LLC
Chambersburg PA
CBHW041809040426
42449CB00001B/32
9780983875703